EXPLORING THE SOLAR SYSTEM

MARS

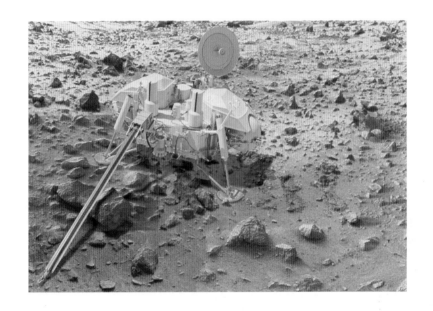

GILES SPARROW

Heinemann
LIBRARY

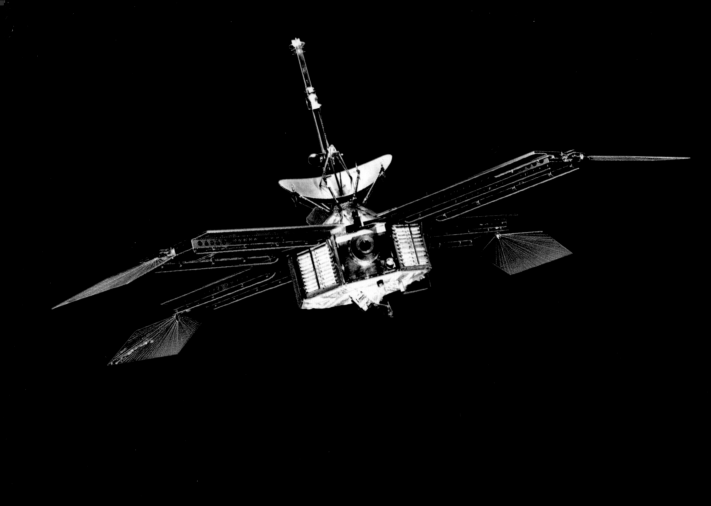

MARS

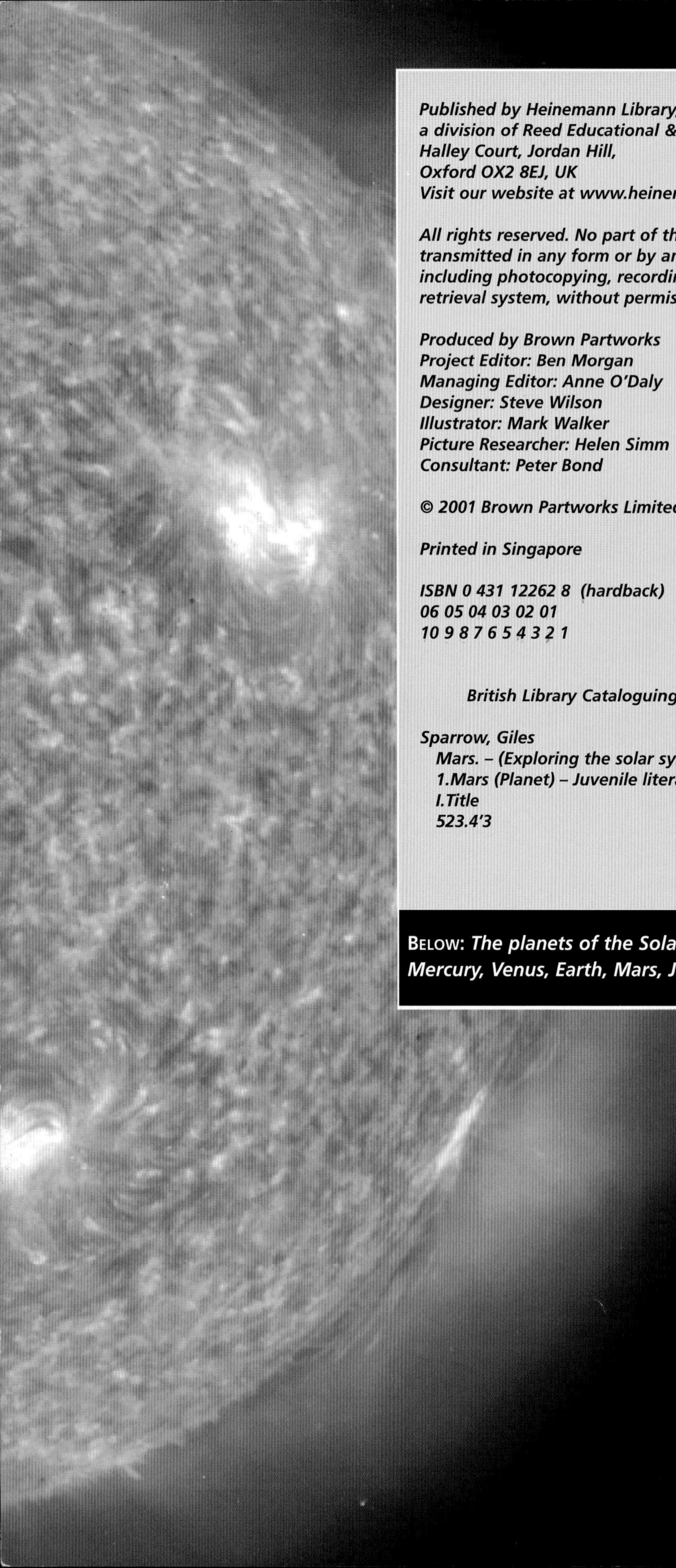

Published by Heinemann Library,
a division of Reed Educational & Professional Publishing,
Halley Court, Jordan Hill,
Oxford OX2 8EJ, UK
Visit our website at www.heinemann.co.uk/library

Produced by Brown Partworks
Project Editor: Ben Morgan
Managing Editor: Anne O'Daly
Designer: Steve Wilson
Illustrator: Mark Walker
Picture Researcher: Helen Simm
Consultant: Peter Bond

© 2001 Brown Partworks Limited

Printed in Singapore

ISBN 0 431 12262 8 (hardback)   ISBN 0 431 12271 7 (paperback)
06 05 04 03 02 01   06 05 04 03 02 01
10 9 8 7 6 5 4 3 2 1   10 9 8 7 6 5 4 3 2 1

British Library Cataloguing in Publication Data

Sparrow, Giles
   Mars. – (Exploring the solar system)
   1.Mars (Planet) – Juvenile literature
   I.Title
   523.4'3

BELOW: *The planets of the Solar System, shown in order from the Sun:*
Mercury, Venus, Earth, Mars, Jupiter, Saturn, Uranus, Neptune, Pluto.

CONTENTS

*Some words are shown in bold, **like this**.
You can find out what they mean by looking in the glossary.*

Where is Mars?

Mars is our next-door neighbour in the Solar System. It is the fourth planet from the Sun, after Mercury, Venus and Earth. Like these other inner planets, Mars is terrestrial, or Earth-like – it is a solid ball made of rock and metal. Beyond Mars lies the **asteroid belt**, a vast ring of huge space boulders. Further still are Jupiter, Saturn, Uranus and Neptune – gigantic planets made of gas and ice.

Mars goes around the Sun in a huge circle called an **orbit**, and the time it takes to complete one orbit is a Martian year. The Martian year is 687 Earth days long, nearly twice as long as our own year. Because its orbit isn't a perfect circle, Mars's distance from the Sun varies during the year. On average it is 228 million kilometres (142 million miles) from the Sun – a distance that would take about 12 years to travel at the speed of Concorde (2179 kilometres per hour or 1354 miles per hour). The distance between Mars and Earth varies enormously because it depends on where the two planets are in their orbits. They are closest when they line up on the same side of the Sun.

Getting to Mars

The time it takes to reach Mars depends on your method of transport, and on the positions of Mars and Earth in their orbits when you set off.

Distance from Earth to Mars

Closest	**56 million km (35 million miles)**
Furthest	**400 million km (248 million miles)**

By car at 113 km per hour (70 miles per hour)

Closest	**57 years**
Furthest	**404 years**

By rocket at 11 km per second (7 miles per second)

Closest	**58 days**
Furthest	**410 days**

Time for radio signals to reach Mars (at the speed of light)

Closest	**3 min. 8 sec.**
Furthest	**22 min. 13 sec.**

Distance from the Sun

The diagram shows how far the planets are from the Sun. Mars is one of the inner planets, along with Earth. Although it looks close to us on this scale, it is millions of kilometres away.

Sun Mercury Venus Earth Mars Jupiter Saturn

0   1000 (621)   2000 (1243)

Distance in millions of kilometres (millions of miles)

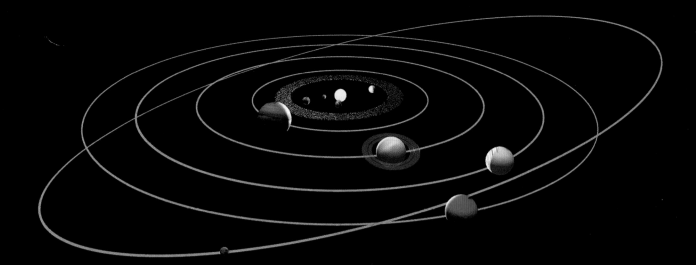

When Earth and Mars line up on the same side of the Sun, astronomers say they are in **opposition**. A trip to Mars at opposition would take only three years at the speed of Concorde. Mars and Earth are furthest when they are on opposite sides of the Sun (**conjunction**) – about 21 years apart at the speed of Concorde.

Missions to Mars have to take the planet's changing orbit into account, so rockets are usually launched when Mars is nearest to Earth. Mars is in this position for just a few months every two years or so.

If **astronauts** ever visit Mars, the vast distance from Earth will make communication with **mission control** difficult. Although radio signals travel at the speed of light, they still take a few minutes to get from Mars to Earth. As a result, astronauts would have to wait at least 6 minutes for a reply when they spoke to mission control, and sometimes for as long as 44 minutes!

The Solar System is made up of the Sun, nine planets and the asteroid belt. The planets go around the Sun in giant circles called orbits.

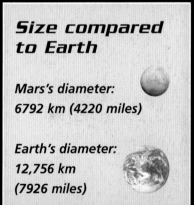

Size compared to Earth

Mars's diameter:
6792 km (4220 miles)

Earth's diameter:
12,756 km
(7926 miles)

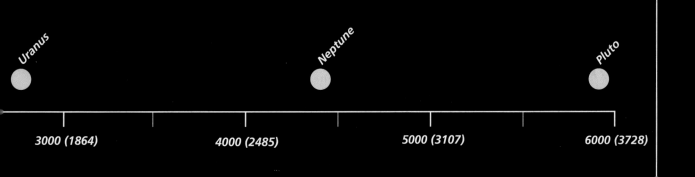

Uranus

Neptune

Pluto

3000 (1864)   4000 (2485)   5000 (3107)   6000 (3728)

First view

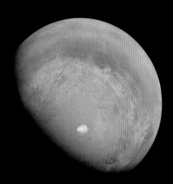

This artist's impression shows a fleet of spaceships setting off for Mars. Astronomers have long dreamed of visiting Mars to find out whether the planet once supported life.

Imagine leaving Earth on a spaceship bound for Mars. The trip will take about a year and half, and you will have to carry enough food and water to last for at least three years to cover your stay on Mars and the return journey.

There is no **gravity** in space, so as soon as you escape Earth's pull you find yourself floating in midair. This strange new sensation doesn't last very long, however. If you were to spend three years in zero-gravity your bones and muscles would waste away through lack of exercise, so your ship starts spinning around to create **artificial gravity**.

From Earth, Mars looks like an orange star. A good telescope will turn it into a tiny reddish disk with a few dark blotches. Astronomers once thought the dark regions were areas of vegetation because they fade and reappear over long periods, just as forests on Earth lose their leaves in winter.

Mars is tiny compared with the vastness of space, so you would have to get close before you could see the planet's circular shape with the naked eye. But on your final approach you would have a breathtaking view. Because your journey takes a curved flight path, not a straight line, you would see something astronomers never see from Earth: Mars seen from the side, a spectacular red **crescent** only partially lit by the Sun.

Getting closer

As you get close to Mars you start to see detail. You can see shades of red and brown, as well as brilliant white patches at the north and south **poles**. Just like Earth, Mars has **polar ice caps** that shrink in summer and expand in winter. Unlike Earth, though, Mars doesn't have a thick, cloudy **atmosphere** to hide the ground. As a result, you can see that the planet's northern and southern halves are different. The south is covered with craters, their rims casting crisp black shadows across the ground, while the north is barren and smooth. But the most spectacular features on Mars are gigantic volcanoes – far bigger than any volcanoes on Earth – and a deep canyon that looks like a gash across the planet's face.

By watching these features appear and disappear as Mars rotates, you calculate the length of a Martian day. It is surprisingly similar to Earth's, at 24 hours and 38 minutes.

Finally, you arrive in **orbit** above Mars. The planet is spread out below you, filling the windows of your ship and throwing an eerie red light into it. Now you can see that Mars does have an atmosphere after all – thin clouds drift over the volcanoes, and mist hangs in the canyon. Time to go down to the surface.

The giant volcanoes on Mars look like a row of black bruises. Their craters are visible from thousands of kilometres away.

What's it like on the surface?

As your spaceship lands, it throws up a cloud of dust, blocking the view through the windows. You wait for the dust to clear before putting on your spacesuit and opening the door for a look outside.

At first glance Mars seems just like a rocky desert on Earth. But then you start noticing differences. For one thing, the sky is pink, except for a few streaks of white cloud. And the ground is not sand-coloured, but reddish-orange. Mars is red because its rocks contain the chemical that forms when iron rusts: iron oxide. In the distance, you might see rolling hills, but there are no mountains.

After climbing to the ground you notice how light you are. Although Mars's weak **gravity** might be a shock after the weightlessness of space travel, you are still only a third of your Earth weight. You can walk more easily than **astronauts** on the Moon could, but if you try running you'll fly into the air with each bound. But it would not be wise to try running on Mars. As far as you can see, the ground is littered with chunks of rock that could trip you. Perhaps they are debris from the distant past, when Mars was pounded by thousands of **asteroids**.

ABOVE: *This artist's impression shows an astronaut on Mars. The spacesuit is essential because Martian air is unbreathable.*

Looking around, you spot several **meteorite** craters. These hollows in the ground are only a few feet across and still sharply defined – they could have been made yesterday. As you step close to one its rim collapses in a cloud of dust, forcing you to jump backwards. The red dust covers everything and kicks up in clouds as you walk. Martian dust is finer than flour, so it hangs in the air for a long time before settling back to the ground.

A wind springs up, flinging dust in your face, but you can barely feel or hear anything. The air is so thin that even a raging gale could not knock you over. And with little air to carry sound, Mars is almost silent. All you can hear is the sound of your breathing inside the spacesuit, as well as the crackle of your headset radio. Something else feels odd. Mars is bitterly cold, so your spacesuit is padded to keep you warm, but even through the suit you feel warm one minute and cold the next. This is because temperatures on the surface can change by up to 20°C (36°F) within a few metres or a few seconds.

Whirlwinds

*Among the hazards that a visitor to Mars would face are ferocious whirlwinds that sweep across the planet like small tornadoes, as in the artist's impression above. They are caused by swirling winds that suck dust up from the ground. The whirlwinds leave looping trails across the surface of Mars that are visible from **orbit**.*

BELOW: *Mars looks like a parched red desert. Even the sky looks red because dust is blown into the air by the Martian winds.*

11

Volcanoes and canyons

The surface of Mars is divided neatly into two areas. In the south there are slightly raised highlands, covered with craters. In the north there are flat plains. Between the two there is a huge bump in the Martian surface, called the Tharsis Rise, home to the huge volcanoes.

The volcanoes are the most spectacular features on Mars. The biggest, Olympus Mons (Mount Olympus), rises 27 kilometres (17 miles) above the Martian surface – three times the height of Mount Everest. Three more volcanoes form a line across the Tharsis Rise, where the planet's surface bulges out by 10 kilometres (6 miles).

The Martian volcanoes oozed lava slowly over millions of years, building up layer after layer with each eruption. Originally the lava came out of a crack in the ground, but as the lava piled up the centre of the volcano collapsed and formed a sunken crater called a **caldera**. The caldera of Olympus Mons is 90 kilometres (56 miles) wide. Today the volcanoes on Mars are silent, and there is no sign of activity that could make them erupt in the future.

Olympus Mons is three times taller than Mount Everest, but it is so wide that you'd hardly notice the slope if you climbed it.

ABOVE RIGHT: *A space probe took this close-up photo of the crater in the volcano Olympus Mons.*

RIGHT: *The Martian volcano Olympus Mons is the biggest volcano in the solar system.*

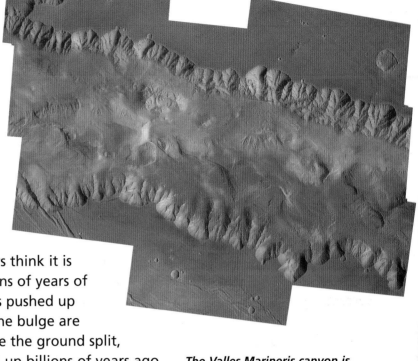

But their surfaces are quite young, suggesting they were active as recently as 150 million years ago. Although this seems like a long time, it is not long enough to tell whether the volcanoes are **extinct** or merely sleeping.

The Tharsis Rise is huge – over 4000 kilometres (2500 miles) across. No one really knows how it formed. Some astronomers think it is just a build-up of lava from billions of years of eruptions, but others think it was pushed up from inside the planet. Around the bulge are huge trenches and canyons where the ground split, perhaps as the bulge was pushed up billions of years ago.

The Valles Marineris canyon is long enough to stretch all the way from London to Baghdad. Its towering cliffs are up to 6 kilometres (4 miles) tall.

The biggest of these canyon systems is the Valles Marineris, a vast, steep-sided gorge that runs for 4000 kilometres (2500 miles) along the Martian **equator**. The Valles Marineris is ten times longer and four times deeper than Earth's Grand Canyon. In fact, it is almost big enough to swallow the entire Himalayan mountain range, although a few peaks would stick out of the top.

Grand Canyon

*Mars's Valles Marineris is often compared to Earth's Grand Canyon (right), but the two canyons formed in very different ways. Valles Marineris formed where the Martian **crust** stretched and split apart, like the Red Sea on Earth. The Grand Canyon was slowly carved out of the ground by the Colorado River.*

Highlands and plains

Apart from the volcanoes, the Martian landscape is dominated by open plains and raised highlands. There are a few **impact craters** across the plains and volcanoes, but most are concentrated in the highlands.

Over billions of years, most of the smaller craters have been worn away, so now only the biggest or most recent craters are obvious. By far the largest is the Hellas basin, which is more than 1800 kilometres (1100 miles) wide and was made by a huge impact late in Mars's formation. The craters on Mars have been slowly worn away by wind and landslides, but some parts of the planet show where another force has been at work – water.

Astronomers think that Mars once had much more water than it does today. Most of it would have collected in the northern plains, which are the lowest part of the surface.

This crater is called Happy Face.

The plains have broad trenches and gullies that seem to have formed in massive floods, perhaps when a lake or sea broke through a natural dam, or when water suddenly erupted from deep underground. Other areas have winding valleys that were slowly worn into the ground by rivers.

By studying the amount of **erosion** caused by water on Mars, astronomers have calculated that there was once enough water to cover the whole planet to a depth of about 0.5 kilometres (0.3 miles).

This false-colour image of Mars shows highlands in red and low ground in blue. The north is much flatter and lower than the south. The white bumps are volcanoes.

plains

volcanoes

highlands

In comparison, Earth's oceans would be 3 kilometres (1.8 miles) deep if our planet was perfectly flat.

One of the biggest mysteries about Mars is just where all its water disappeared to, but there is some evidence that water occasionally flows on Mars even today. For instance, some Martian craters have small gullies in their rims, where water appears to have briefly flowed downhill, perhaps after seeping out from underground.

Millions of years ago, water flowed along this Martian river valley and drained into the crater at the northern end, where there may have been a lake.

Dating the surface

*In the early days of the Solar System, the planets were bombarded with millions of **asteroids** and **comets**, and Mars would have been covered with craters. Since then, geological processes slowly resurfaced the planet and wiped away its oldest craters.*

Astronomers can calculate how old the resurfaced areas are by counting how many new craters have appeared in them. Comet and asteroid impacts happen at a steady rate, so the density of craters gives a fairly accurate measure of age.

The northern plains have the fewest craters, so they must be the youngest areas of Mars. Perhaps the plains formed in the same way as the 'seas' on our Moon – from huge floods of lava that spread over wide areas.

The polar caps

The north and south **poles** of Mars are covered by thin ice caps that expand and contract with the seasons. Although from Earth they look like our own planet's **polar ice caps**, they are actually very different.

The main difference is that Mars's ice caps are mostly frozen **carbon dioxide**, the main gas in Martian air; only the **north pole** has water ice. On Earth frozen carbon dioxide is used to make dry ice, which turns from a solid into a gas without having to be liquid in between, and this is what seems to happen on Mars. When it is summer in Mars's northern hemisphere, heat from the Sun makes the northern ice cap shrink. Meanwhile it is winter in the south, and the southern ice cap expands as the carbon dioxide air freezes on top of and around it.

Astronomers hope that the presence of water in the northern ice cap is a sign that more water ice is trapped below the Martian surface. One day, the climate may change enough for this underground ice to melt again.

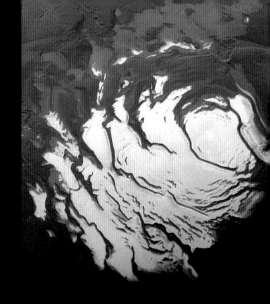

ABOVE: *The swirling pattern of ice at the **south pole** may be caused by Martian winds.*

BELOW: *This 3-D view of the north pole was made from data sent back to Earth from a **space probe**.*

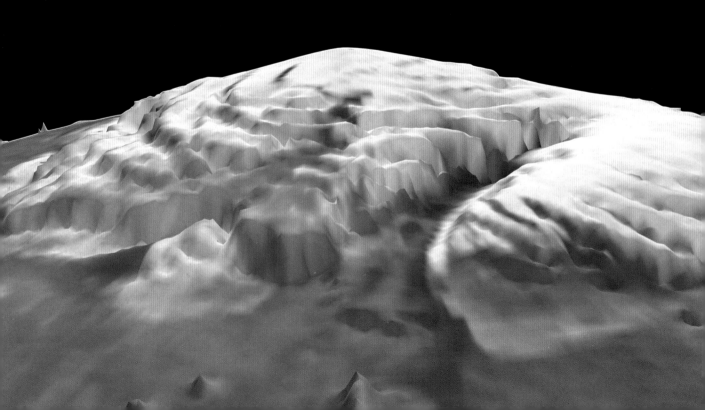

What is Mars made of?

If you could split Mars open, you would see three separate layers inside the planet. The thin, solidified surface is called the **crust**. Below the crust is the **mantle**, which is more than 1600 kilometres (1000 miles) deep. The rock in the mantle is very hot and moves around slowly like a thick, syrupy liquid. In the middle of the planet is the **core** – a gigantic ball of iron.

Astronomers don't know how big the core is or whether it is molten like Earth's, or solid. One clue comes from the fact that Mars has no **magnetic field**. Earth's strong magnetism is caused by molten iron spinning in the core as the planet rotates. Perhaps the reason that Mars has no magnetism is because its iron core has long since frozen.

The rocks that make up Mars are something of a mystery. In theory, all the rocky inner planets – Mercury, Venus, Earth and Mars – should have the same composition. But **space probes** that have landed on Mars have shown that it is less dense than Earth, and its surface rocks contain less iron than Earth's rocks and more of the mineral silica.

Most Martian rock seems to be **igneous**: it formed from molten rock that solidified as it cooled. However, space probes have seen horizontal lines on Martian hillsides that suggest there might be sedimentary rocks too, a clue that Mars once had water. Sedimentary rocks form when sand or mud sinks to a sea floor and becomes compressed

crust

mantle

core

Mars is made of three layers, like Earth: a crust, a mantle and a core. The mantle is probably hot and molten, but the crust consists of solid rock. No one knows for sure what the core is like.

How did Mars form?

Mars formed 4.5 billion years ago from a cloud of gas and dust that surrounded a newly born star – the Sun. All the planets in the Solar System formed in a similar way, as flecks of material in the dust cloud collided and stuck together until they had enough **gravity** to start pulling in material. The frequent collisions made the growing clumps of material, or **planetesimals**, get so hot that they melted and re-formed into balls. As the rock melted, heavy **elements** sank to the centre and light elements rose to the surface. As a result, Mars ended up with a central **core** of iron, overlaid by a **mantle** of semi-molten rock and topped by a solid **crust**, just like Earth. Because Mars was smaller than Earth it cooled down more quickly – just as a cup of hot water gets cold more quickly than a bath.

This artist's impression shows what a violent place the young Solar System was. Swirling clouds of debris and comets surrounded the Sun, which itself formed in a colossal nuclear reaction.

On Earth the crust formed slowly and split into huge slabs, called **plates**. Over millions of years, these drifted around Earth's surface, floating on the semi-liquid mantle beneath and carrying the continents with them. Mars never formed plates, so its surface has not moved for a very long time.

The lack of plates explains many Martian features. Earth's mountains are mostly produced by collisions between plates, so because Mars has no plates it has no mountains. Its volcanoes have grown huge because they have been erupting in the same place for billions of years.

But this is only part of the story. Astronomers now know that Mars has a thicker, lumpier crust under the southern highlands than beneath the northern plains. They think this is because the southern crust cooled quickly and solidified before it had time to flatten. The northern plains stayed molten longer and so became smoother.

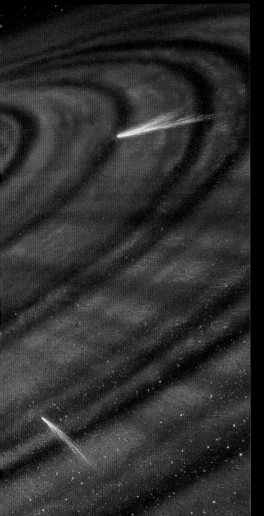

The different rates of cooling might have been caused by a large planetesimal hitting the northern half of Mars and generating a lot of heat. As well as making the crust flatter, the collision would have melted **meteorite** craters and made the ground smooth.

The early Mars was very different from the planet we know today. Water vapour and **carbon dioxide** escaping from volcanoes would have given Mars a thick **atmosphere** like Earth's, and the water would have rained down from the sky to form oceans, lakes and rivers.

How stars form

Stars and planets are born inside interstellar gas clouds called nebulas, such as the Eagle Nebula (above). At the top of the Eagle Nebula, gravity is making gas and dust shrink into finger-shaped blobs. Eventually the contracting gas will get so hot and dense that it will turn into stars and planets. Each finger is big enough to swallow our Solar System.

Weather and climate

Mars is a freezing desert, with dry and bitterly cold weather. The gas **carbon dioxide**, which we breathe out as a waste product, makes up 95 percent of the air. At this level carbon dioxide is deadly – you would suffocate if you tried breathing it. However, Martian air is 100 times less **dense** than Earth's air, so it would be too thin to breathe. To remove your spacesuit helmet for just seconds would be lethal. Because of the low air pressure, the liquid in your eyes would boil and your blood would turn into froth and fill your lungs with foam, drowning you.

The sky on Mars is usually clear and pink, but sometimes small white clouds appear, mostly around the **poles** in winter or near the **equator** in summer.

Blown away

*Long ago Mars was covered by a thick **atmosphere**, but for some reason it lost most of its air. Perhaps the air was blasted off the planet by **asteroid** impacts or blown away by radiation from the Sun. After losing its air Mars grew cold and its water mostly disappeared.*

The clouds are made of crystals of water ice and frozen carbon dioxide, and they are always thin and wispy. There is nothing as dark and heavy as storm clouds on Earth. Some of the clouds form over volcanoes. As air flows over the volcanoes it is pushed up to a higher and colder level, where it forms ice crystals.

Strong winds often sweep across the surface of Mars, whipping up dust into vast clouds hundreds of kilometres wide. These dust storms would be terrifying to get caught in – the Sun would disappear in a blinding haze, and you would completely lose sight of your spaceship. Some Martian dust storms spread out to cover the entire planet for weeks on end, particularly when Mars is closest to the Sun.

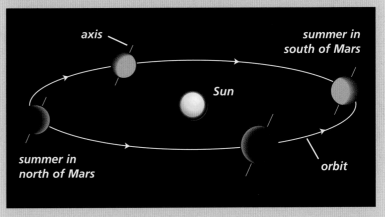

ABOVE: *Mars's hazy air is visible over the horizon in this photo from a Viking space probe.*

BELOW LEFT: *The raging dust storms that sometimes envelop Mars are caused by violent winds.*

Martian seasons

*Like Earth, Mars spins on a tilted **axis**, and this causes seasons. When the **north pole** is tilted towards the Sun, it is summer in the north and winter in the south. When the **south pole** is tilted towards the Sun, it is summer in the south and winter in the north.*

Because the Martian year is about twice the length of an Earth year, seasons on Mars last much longer than on Earth. The tilt of Mars's axis varies gradually over time, meaning that Mars sometimes has much more extreme seasons.

axis

summer in south of Mars

Sun

summer in north of Mars

orbit

A typical day

You decide to spend a whole day on Mars, so you land your ship on the dark side of the planet just before dawn. Outside, the nighttime temperature is a chilly –125°C (–193°F) and a layer of frost covers the ground. When the Sun rises and the sky begins to turn pink, the temperature slowly rises to about freezing point. As the first rays of sunlight hit the ground, the frost evaporates, but it then condenses almost immediately in the cold air, forming a sheet of white mist that floats over the ground.

The Martian day is 24 hours and 38 minutes long – about the same as Earth's – and the Sun moves through the sky at about the same speed as on Earth. As the Sun climbs high, the morning mist dissolves and a wind whips up. Small whirlwinds, or dust devils, swirl across the plain in the distance, throwing fountains of pink dust into the air.

In the evening, hazy clouds start to form. The Sun sinks low on the horizon and turns blue as the **atmosphere** filters out its red light. Finally, it disappears behind rolling hills, and night returns. In the darkening sky you see two faint stars, actually Mars's moons. One moves rapidly across the sky – it circles the planet in less than eight hours. The other moves so slowly that it seems rooted to the spot.

ABOVE: *Martian mornings are often frosty. The frost is made of ice crystals that fall to the ground during the freezing night.*

BELOW: *Martian sunsets are the opposite of Earth sunsets. On Earth, the blue sky turns red around the setting Sun, but on Mars the red sky turns blue.*

Martian meteorites

Astronomers don't yet have bits of Martian rock collected by **astronauts** or **space probes**, but they do have the next best thing – little bits of Mars found lying around on Earth.

These rocks arrive as **meteorites** – large shooting stars that make it all the way to the Earth's surface without burning up. Most meteorites are just debris left over from the formation of the Solar System, but a few show signs that they formed inside planets, where high pressure can heat, melt and change them.

ABOVE: *Very rarely, Martian rocks land on Earth as meteorites. Only fifteen have been found so far.*

When Martian meteorites were first discovered in the 1980s, scientists compared the gases trapped inside them to the composition of the Martian atmosphere and found that they matched. The meteorites must have been blasted off Mars in huge collisions millions of years ago.

BELOW: *Could these microscopic structures on meteorite ALH84001 be fossils of Martian bacteria?*

The best-known Martian meteorite is ALH84001, which was found in Antarctica in 1984. In 1996 NASA experts announced that this rock contained signs of Martian life-forms, including strange structures that looked like bacteria. However, many scientists now think these are just mineral patterns in the rock.

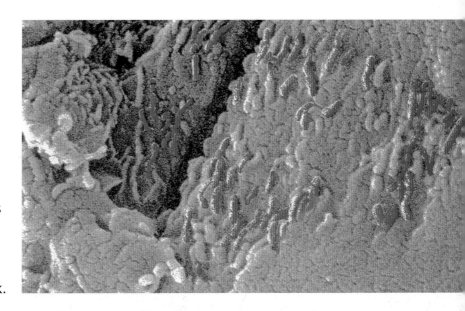

Moons of Mars

Mars has two tiny moons, named Phobos and Deimos (fear and panic) after the companions of Ares, the Greek god of war. Each moon is an uneven lump of rock just a few miles across.

The moons were discovered by Asaph Hall, an astronomer from the USA. Hall had calculated that Mars ought to have at least one moon, and he set out to look for it using the US Naval Observatory's telescopes when Mars came close to Earth in 1877. Eventually Hall found two moons, but they were much smaller and closer to Mars than he had expected.

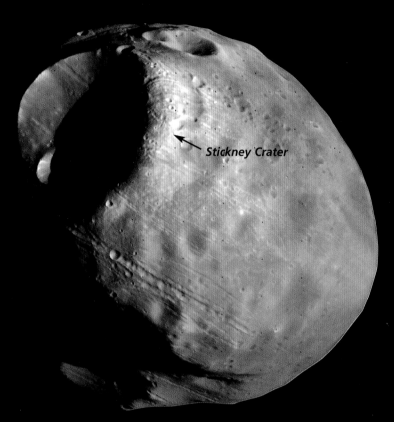

Stickney Crater

Phobos is the bigger of Mars's two moons.

Deimos, the outer moon, is just 15 kilometres (9 miles) wide. It **orbits** Mars once every 30 hours, only 20,000 kilometres (12,400 miles) above the Martian surface – a tiny distance compared to the 378,000 kilometres (234,900 miles) between Earth and our own Moon.

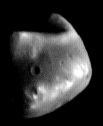

Deimos

Phobos is larger and even closer to Mars. It is 28 kilometres (17 miles) long and dominated by a 10-kilometre (6-mile) crater. The crater is named Stickney after Asaph Hall's wife, Angelina Stickney Hall, who encouraged him in his search. Phobos takes just 7 hours 40 minutes to orbit Mars at a height of only 6000 kilometres (3700 miles), and it is so close to the planet that its orbit is unstable. Phobos is gradually getting closer and closer to Mars. Eventually it will smash into the planet and be destroyed.

When the Viking **space probes** visited Mars in the 1970s, scientists discovered that these moons are very different from other moons in the Solar System.

They are too small to have a regular shape, and both of them have a very dark surface, perhaps caused by some sort of dark mineral coating the rocky core. These features suggest that the moons are really **asteroids** that were captured by Mars's **gravity** early in the planet's history.

One failed attempt to learn more about the moons was the Phobos missions. Two Soviet space probes were launched in 1988, but they were lost before they reached their target. If they had arrived safely they would have dropped **landers** onto the moons to analyse the rocks.

This artist's impression shows one of the ill-fated Phobos probes that were sent to study Mars's biggest moon.

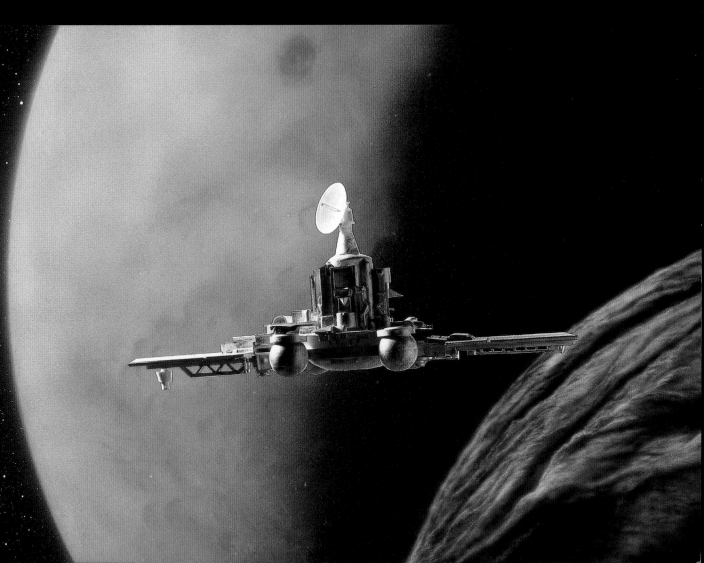

Stories and myths

Mars is named after the Roman god of war, but it has had many other names in the past. The ancient Egyptians called it Har Decher, meaning the red one. In 400 BC astonomers from Babylon, in what is now Iraq, called Mars Nergal after a legendary warrior hero. This was probably the first time that the angry red colour of Mars was linked to war. The Greeks called the planet Ares, after their god of war, and this became Mars under the Romans.

Some of the best science-fiction stories have been about Mars or Martians. *The War of the Worlds* (1898) by H.G. Wells tells the story of a Martian invasion of Earth in the 1890s. Wells's strange, tentacled Martians were fearsome enemies, equipped with armoured ships and heat rays. The book inspired films, a musical and, most famously, a radio version. This was broadcast in the USA on Halloween night in 1938. It featured a fake news bulletin that was so realistic that thousands of people panicked, thinking a Martian invasion was really happening.

Before the first **space probes** were sent to Mars, writers visited the planet in their imaginations. Edgar Rice Burroughs, the inventor of Tarzan, wrote a series of books about a man who was magically swept away to become Warlord of Mars.

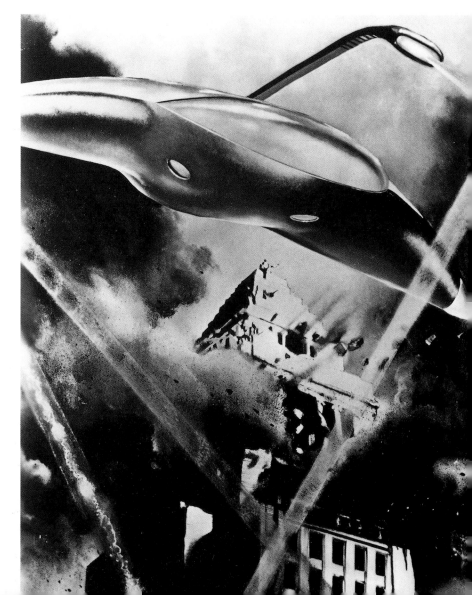

Martian spaceships attack Earth in a 1953 film version of H.G. Wells's The War of the Worlds*. The film's director changed the setting from Victorian England to the USA of the 1950s.*

RIGHT: *Humans meet the Martian emperor in the film* Mars Attacks.

BELOW: *The Romans named Mars after their god of war, perhaps because of its blood-red colour.*

In the 1950s, authors linked Mars to the threat of communism. Countless books and films about Martians were really expressions of fear of a Russian invasion. The 1996 film *Mars Attacks* is a spoof of these stories.

In the 1960s, space probes showed Mars to be a lifeless desert and so brought an end to stories of little green men. More recent books have explored how people might colonize Mars and make it like Earth, as in Kim Stanley Robinson's trilogy *Red Mars*, *Green Mars* and *Blue Mars*.

The face on Mars

In 1976 a space probe photographed what appeared to be a giant human face on Mars (left). Some people thought it might be a statue carved by aliens or by an ancient Martian civilization. However, pictures taken by another probe in 1998 showed that the face was just an illusion.

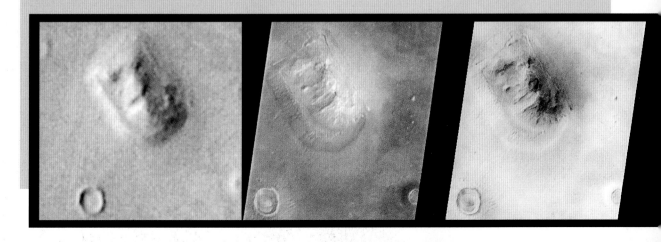

Early discoveries

People have been using telescopes to look at Mars since the 1600s, but the early telescopes were too small to see detail. The first person to record markings on the surface of Mars was Dutch astronomer Christiaan Huygens, who saw a large, dark triangle on the planet in 1659. By watching this disappear and reappear, Huygens calculated the length of a Martian day.

Huygens was also the first to notice a white spot at the Martian **south pole**, but it wasn't until 1704 that the Italian astronomer Giancomo Miraldi noticed a similar spot at the **north pole**. Miraldi correctly guessed that the white spots were ice caps.

William Herschel (1738–1822), the German musician and amateur astronomer who discovered Uranus, was also interested in Mars. He saw that stars did not fade as they passed behind the edge of Mars, and so he deduced that the Martian **atmosphere** had to be thin. Herschel thought the dark patches on Mars were oceans. However, later astronomers noticed that the patches changed shape through the year and so suggested they were vegetation. The dark areas seemed to grow as the polar caps shrank, as though the melting ice was watering the plants. We now know that the changing shapes are just caused by dust blowing off the darker rock beneath.

In 1877 the Italian astronomer Giovanni Schiaparelli published the first detailed map of the surface of Mars. This map caused a lot of trouble.

Astronomer William Herschel's sister Caroline dutifully recorded all his observations.

Christiaan Huygens
(1629–1693)

An astronomer, physicist, mathematician and inventor, the Dutch scientist Christiaan Huygens was a success in many fields. Like many early astronomers, he built his own telescopes. His discoveries included the dark zones on Mars and the true shape of Saturn's rings. Huygens also founded the wave theory of light.

ABOVE: *Percival Lowell's observatory at Flagstaff, Arizona, USA, is still in use today.*

Schiaparelli drew a series of fine lines between the dark zones. He thought the lines were rivers between areas of vegetation, so he labelled them *canali*, the Italian word for channels.

But *canali* was translated as canals, which means artificial waterways. This caused huge arguments because it implied that Mars had once been home to an advanced civilization. Many people insisted they could see the canals when they looked through telescopes, but others thought the canals were an illusion. The controversy raged until the first **space probes** sent back clear photographs of Mars. People then realized that they had been fooled into seeing what they wanted to see.

Missions to Mars

When astronomers began sending probes into space in the 1950s, Mars was an obvious target because many people thought it might support life. The Soviet Union launched its first **space probe** to Mars in 1960, but the craft never left Earth's **orbit**. NASA then took the lead with the Mariner **missions**.

The first successful Mars probe was *Mariner 4*, which was launched in November 1964 and flew past Mars in July 1965. The probe got within 9600 kilometres (6000 miles) of the surface, giving astronomers their first good look at the planet. *Mariner 4* sent back 21 pictures of the cratered southern half of Mars and found that the planet did not have a strong **magnetic field** like Earth's, or a thick **atmosphere**.

Four years later, *Mariners 6* and *7* arrived at Mars. These probes were much more sophisticated – they analysed chemicals in the atmosphere and ice caps and took close-up photographs of the surface. Although the missions were a success, many people were disappointed. The probes were revealing a dead world more like the Moon than Earth. The thin air was unbreathable, and the **polar ice caps** were mostly frozen **carbon dioxide** rather than water ice. The surface pictures showed a barren desert covered with craters.

Lift-off! It took a huge rocket to launch Mariner 6. *The probe took 75 pictures of Mars and then disappeared into deep space.*

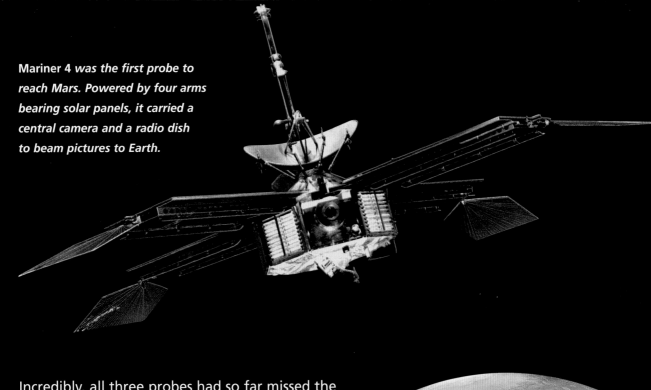

Mariner 4 *was the first probe to reach Mars. Powered by four arms bearing solar panels, it carried a central camera and a radio dish to beam pictures to Earth.*

Incredibly, all three probes had so far missed the volcanoes, canyons and river valleys. The early Mariner missions were flybys. The probes spent just a few hours monitoring Mars as they flew past. The next probe, *Mariner 9*, went into orbit around Mars and photographed it for several months.

Mariner 9 was launched in May 1971 to take advantage of Mars's closest approach to Earth, but when it reached Mars in November the whole planet was covered by a dust storm. Gradually the view cleared, and *Mariner 9* began to send back photographs that revealed for the first time the complex and varied nature of the Martian surface. The probe was designed to work for three months but it operated successfully for nearly a year. Finally it ran out of fuel and began to tumble towards Mars, trapped by **gravity**. As a memorial, the Valles Marineris canyon was named in honour of this pioneering spacecraft.

Viking probes

The success of *Mariner 9* triggered renewed interest in Mars, and NASA began planning its next **missions** – ambitious **space probes** that would **orbit** Mars for years and send robot **landers** to the surface.

The Soviet Union had already tried to send robot landers to Mars but was still having bad luck. Its *Mars 2* and *3* probes arrived in 1971 during the same planet-wide dust storm that greeted *Mariner 9*. Unfortunately the landing sequence could not be delayed, and the landers disappeared into the storm. One was never heard of again. The other landed successfully but stopped working after only 20 seconds.

The two Viking probes were launched by NASA in August and September 1975 and established orbit around Mars in mid-1976. Each probe consisted of an **orbiter** and a lander joined together. Once the probes were in orbit, the landers were released to make their perilous descent by parachute onto the rock-strewn surface hundreds of miles below. Meanwhile the orbiters continued to circle Mars, taking thousands of photographs.

Viking 2 was launched by rocket in September 1975 and took eleven months to reach Mars.

The *Viking 1* lander touched down on 20 July 1976 in a region called Chryse Planitia (the Plains of Gold).

Touchdown on Mars

The Viking 1 *lander separated from its orbiter on July 20, 1976 while orbiting Mars at around 10,500 kilometres per hour (6500 miles per hour). The lander fired its braking rockets, causing it to fall to a lower orbit. After settling at the new orbit, it fired the braking rockets again and, protected by a heat shield, it began its plunge into the Martian **atmosphere**. Within a matter of minutes, air resistance had slowed the craft to a mere 900 kilometres per hour (560 miles per hour). At a height of about 6 kilometres (4 miles), the lander released parachutes and jettisoned the heat shield. When it reached a height of 1.6 kilometres (1 mile), the rockets gave a final burst, slowing the fall enough to allow a gentle touchdown. The rockets were designed to avoid burning the ground directly below the lander, where scientists wanted to analyse the dirt and rocks.*

It sent back the first pictures from the surface, causing huge excitement. The pictures revealed a rocky desert landscape and pink skies. *Viking 2* followed on 3 September, landing 6700 kilometres (4040 miles) away on Utopia Planitia (the Plains of Utopia).

The landers carried cameras, weather instruments, earthquake detectors and **magnetic field** detectors. Both had a robot arm to pick up dirt and an onboard laboratory to analyse the dirt for chemical signs of life. One experiment added water to a dirt sample to see if it caused a chemical reaction. Another looked to see if the soil absorbed or released gases when exposed to sunlight, and a third injected nutrients into the soil to see if there was a reaction. Although the results were interesting, the experiments failed to find any evidence of life.

ABOVE: *The Viking probes gave us our first view of Mars's surface.*

BELOW: *This artist's impression shows the robot arm scratching a dirt sample from the ground.*

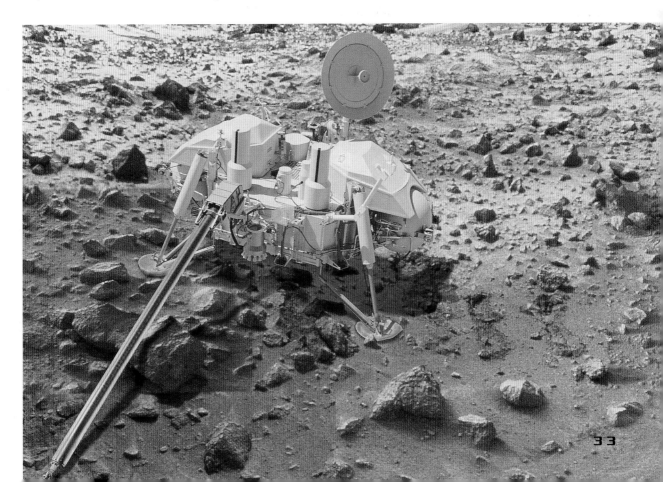

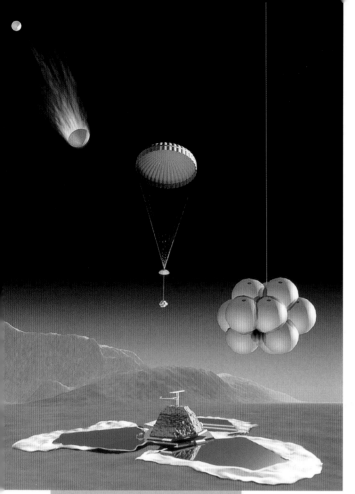

Later missions

There was a long gap after the Viking programme before the next successful **mission** to Mars. In fact it started to seem as though Mars exploration was cursed. The Soviet Union had a series of three failed missions in the 1980s and 1990s, and NASA lost a spacecraft in 1993. But robot explorers eventually returned to Mars in style – with NASA's *Mars Pathfinder* and *Mars Global Surveyor* missions.

Mars Global Surveyor (*MGS*) was launched in November 1996, and *Mars Pathfinder* in December. However, *Pathfinder* got to Mars first, in July 1997, on a shorter **flight path**. *Pathfinder* was a **lander**, while *MGS* was an **orbiter**.

Once on the surface of Mars, *Pathfinder*'s solar panels folded out like petals, providing the lander with power. Its instruments included a weather station, equipment to analyse chemicals in the soil and **magnetic field** sensors. Most importantly, though, it released a remote-controlled buggy called the Sojourner rover, which was about the size of a large microwave oven. The rover trundled around the nearby landscape for almost three months, photographing rocks and analysing them with its chemical sniffers. Cameras mounted in pairs on Sojourner and *Pathfinder* enabled them to produce spectacular 3-D images of the Martian landscape. The mission was a huge success, and millions of people back on Earth watched Sojourner's travels by visiting the *Pathfinder* website.

Meanwhile *MGS* arrived in **orbit** in September 1997 and began to compile a detailed photographic survey of Mars. Its discoveries included dust devils, landslides, evidence that Mars once had a magnetic field and signs of recent flowing water on the surface.

Bouncedown on Mars

Pathfinder *made a very unusual landing on Mars. First it ploughed through the* atmosphere, *protected by a heat shield. Then it released a parachute to slow its fall. To cushion the landing it filled a set of bouncing airbags with gas – the lander bounced fifteen times before rolling to a stop. Finally, the airbags deflated and the solar panels folded open to provide power.*

After descending Pathfinder's ramp, the Sojourner rover began exploring the Martian surface. An intelligent navigation system and cameras enabled it to find its way around independently.

Mars Global Surveyor *has taken thousands of photographs of Mars since it arrived in orbit in September 1997.*

Scientists back on Earth studied how *MGS*'s orbit changed as it went around the planet. These small changes, caused by variations in Mars's **gravity**, revealed that the planet's **crust** was much thicker in the southern hemisphere.

The curse of Mars struck again when NASA's next two missions to Mars – *Mars Climate Orbiter* and *Mars Polar Lander* – both failed in 1999. The *Climate Orbiter* was lost because of a programming error: one ground team was measuring distances in kilometres and metres, and another was using miles and feet!

But the programme to explore Mars is still pushing ahead. The next NASA mission, *Mars Surveyor*, will consist of an orbiter, a lander and a rover vehicle. The European Space Agency has a *Mars Express* mission scheduled for early in the 21st century. This lander-orbiter mission will look for evidence of water hidden beneath the Martian surface. After that, there are even more ambitious plans to send sample-return probes to Mars. These will land, collect rocks and dust and then take off again to bring the samples back to Earth.

Could humans live there?

The first human colonists would have to live in an artificial environment and wear spacesuits whenever they went outdoors.

Of all the planets in the Solar System besides Earth, Mars is the one where humans could live most easily. NASA hopes to send **astronauts** to Mars within the next 20 years. Unlike the astronauts who took part in the Apollo **missions** to the Moon, astronauts travelling to Mars would have to stay on the planet for at least 18 months until Earth was close enough for the return journey.

This ambitious mission will require a lot of planning, and it will be easier if the astronauts do not have to take all their supplies with them. Future **space probes** will try to identify deposits of underground ice that astronauts could use for water or to make oxygen, and NASA's *Mars Surveyor 2001* will carry out experiments to see if fuel for the return trip could be made on Mars.

So when humans go to Mars, they will probably be going to stay. In the long term, it might be possible to make Mars like Earth by pumping gases into its **atmosphere** so that the planet gets warmer. If the ice melted and water started flowing, plants could be grown, and these would slowly turn the **carbon dioxide** air into breathable oxygen. Eventually, after hundreds of years, colonists might be able to walk on Mars without spacesuits. Perhaps they would be the first true Martians.

Glossary

artificial gravity force generated by a spaceship that enables astronauts to stand on the floor instead of floating in midair

asteroid large chunk of rock left over from when the planets formed

asteroid belt ring of asteroids that orbit the Sun between the orbits of Mars and Jupiter

astronaut person trained to go into space

atmosphere layer of gas trapped by gravity around the surface of a planet

axis imaginary line through the middle of a planet that the planet spins around

caldera large crater at the top of a volcano, usually formed by collapse of the cone

carbon dioxide most common gas in the Martian atmosphere, also found as ice at the Martian poles

comet large chunk of ice left over from when the planets formed

conjunction appearance of two planets or a planet and the Sun at the same point in the sky, as seen from Earth. Mars is furthest from Earth when it is in conjunction with the Sun.

core centre of a planet, where the heaviest elements have collected

crescent curved shape like one segment of an orange

crust solid, outer surface of a planet, where the light elements have collected

dense having a lot of weight squeezed into a small space

element chemical that cannot be split into other chemicals. All matter is made of elements.

ellipse stretched circle or oval

equator imaginary line around the centre of a planet, midway between the poles

erosion (weathering) gradual break-up of rock by chemical processes and the action of wind and water.

extinct completely dead; no longer active

flight path route a spacecraft takes to its destination

gas giant huge planet made out of gas. Jupiter, Saturn, Uranus and Neptune are gas giants.

gravity force that pulls objects together. The heavier or closer an object is, the stronger its gravity.

igneous type of rock formed from molten rock (magma) that has cooled and solidified

impact crater circular crater made when an asteroid, comet or meteorite smashes into a planet

lander spacecraft that lands on a planet's surface

magnetic field region around a planet where a compass can detect the north pole

mantle part of a planet between the core and the crust

meteorite rock from space that falls onto the surface of a planet

mission expedition to visit a specific target in space, such as a planet or moon

mission control base on Earth where scientists monitor a spacecraft's progress

north pole point on a planet's surface that coincides with the top end of the planet's axis

opposition appearance of a planet in exactly the opposite direction to the Sun, as seen from Earth. Mars is closest to Earth when it is in opposition with the Sun.

orbit path an object takes around another when it is trapped by the larger object's gravity; or, to take such a path

orbiter spacecraft that orbits a planet

particle tiny fragment of an atom. Particle can also mean a speck of dust or dirt.

planetesimal small body that formed in the early Solar System

plate part of a planet's crust that moves around and collides with other plates

polar ice cap cold area around the pole of a planet where ice collects

pole top or bottom of a planet

sedimentary type of rock that forms when eroded material piles up and compresses

south pole point on a planet's surface that coincides with the bottom end of the planet's axis

space probe robotic vehicle sent from Earth to study the Solar System

Books and websites

Bergreen, Laurence, *The Quest for Mars (NASA Scientists and Their Search for Life Beyond Earth)*. London: HarperCollins Publishers, 2000.

Couper, Heather, and Henbest, Nigel. *The DK Space Encyclopedia.* London: Dorling Kindersley, 1999.

Englebert, Phyllis. *The Handy Space Answer Book*. London: The Gale Group, 1997.

Furniss, Tim. *The Solar System – Spinning Through Space*. London: Hodder Wayland (Hodder & Stoughton Children's Division), 1999.

Kerrod, Robin. *Our Solar System – Near Planets*. London: Belitha Press Ltd, 2000.

cmex-www.arc.nasa.gov – CMEX NASA Ames Space Science Division

mars.jpl.nasa.gov – Mars Exploration Program

www.iag.net/~crs/mars – The Mars Internet Mission

www.marsnews.com – NewsWire for the New Frontier

www.mars-watch.com – The Site for Mars Enthusiasts

Index

Picture Credits
Key: t – top, b – below, c – centre, l – left, r – right. **NASA**: 4–5b, 8tc, 8tr, 9b, 10–11, 12t, 12b, 15, 16t, 16b, 19, 21, 22t, 22b, 24t, 24b, 32, 35t, 35b, Mary A. Dale-Bannister/Washington University 33t, JPL/California Institute of Technology 2, 31t, JPL/Malin Space Science Systems 14t, 27b, Steve Lee (University of Colorado)/Jim Bell (Cornell University)/Mike Wolff (Space Science Institute) 9t; **SOHO***: 4l; **The Art Archive**: 27tl; **Kobal Collection**: Paramount 26, Warner Bros 27tr; **Life File**: Andrew Ward 13b; **Science Photo Library**: 1, 28t, 28b, 29b, 32b, Julian Baum 34, Julian Brown 25, Lynette Cook 18, Tony & Daphne Hallas 29t, David A. Hardy 8, Mehau Kulyk 11t, NASA 14b, 23b, 30b, David Nunuk 23t, Ludek Pesek 20, US Geological Survey 3, 13t, 31b, Detlev Van Ravenswaay 36, Victor Habbick Visions 10t. Front Cover: NASA. Back Cover: NASA, JPL/California Institute of Technology.
*SOHO is a project of international cooperation between ESA & NASA.